Co-creator Note:

I am a Yankee at heart. I love multitasking. When I need to learn something in Photoshop, I "trick" myself by drawing something I love. Painting is not the same as drawing for me, swaths of color as opposed to figuring line weights and the strength of the stroke. I also hear on a regular basis: "I wish I could draw!" The uncharitble thing to say would be "No you don't. It takes hours, days, weeks, years of dedication and applied knowledge to learn, if you really did want to do this, you would start right now." But I understand, most people are talked out of their creativity at a rather early age, for whatever reason and become intimidated at the thought of creating anything to do with art.

By doing something that feeds your soul, you de-stress. Doing something you can look at and like, honoring the artist within you, builds positive feelings. Many have rediscovered the joy of applying color to images. I love the collaborative, unique nature of coloring books. Truly no two people will color the same, so the colorist brings their own flair.

You can play. Use fantastic colors or media. Or you can figure out color theory with no one watching (and Youtube and books hold a great wealth of information). You can show people or keep it a secret pleasure. This book is designed with single-sided images, so you may cut it out and display (and I recommend you do, if you use wet media or markers). Cut it out carefully with an X-acto and ruler, attach to a board with low tack tape and do not remove until our piece is finished and dry.

You could even feel free to scan it and share it with me and the world. I'm starting a coloring fanpage on Facebook, I will announce it on my fan page (https://www.facebook.com/agywilsonwork), if you'd like to share your efforts. There are a couple of pages with nothing on them so you can try whatever media you color with to see how the paper holds up or what the colors look like. Most of all, I hope you enjoy my efforts as well as your own. If you like my work, appreciate this book, I hope you take the time to write a short review and check out my other books. Thank you!

Liberties were taken. Some of the places are very accurate, and others completely thrown together in my head:

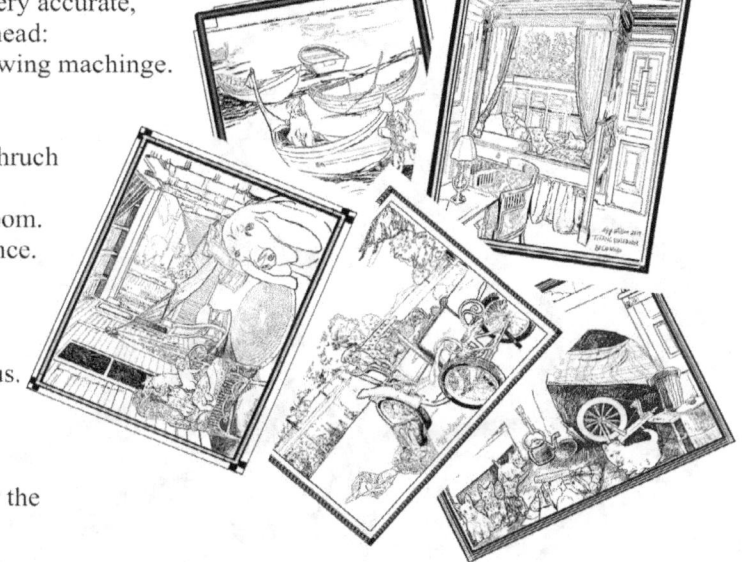

* Kittens in a basket with an old Singer s sewing machince.
* Pugs in a kitchen circa 1735.
* Corgie pups in Titanic stateroom.
* Borzoi pups in the library of the Grand Chruch of the Russian Winterpalace.
* Mau kittens in an Egyptian palace bath room.
* Pomeranian pups at the Ritz Carlton, France.
* Portuguese water puppies in the port.
* Persian kittens in an Iranian house.
* Havanese pups and cat in old Cuba.
* Alaskan Eskimo pus at an old-timey circus.
* An old hound and kittens on a porch.
* Skye Terriers in an old croft house.
* Siamese kittens on a street in Thailand.
* St. Bernard pups in a cottage overlooking the Matterhorn.
* Great Dane pups in the palace at Knossos.
* German Shepherd pups in a Phaetonnette.

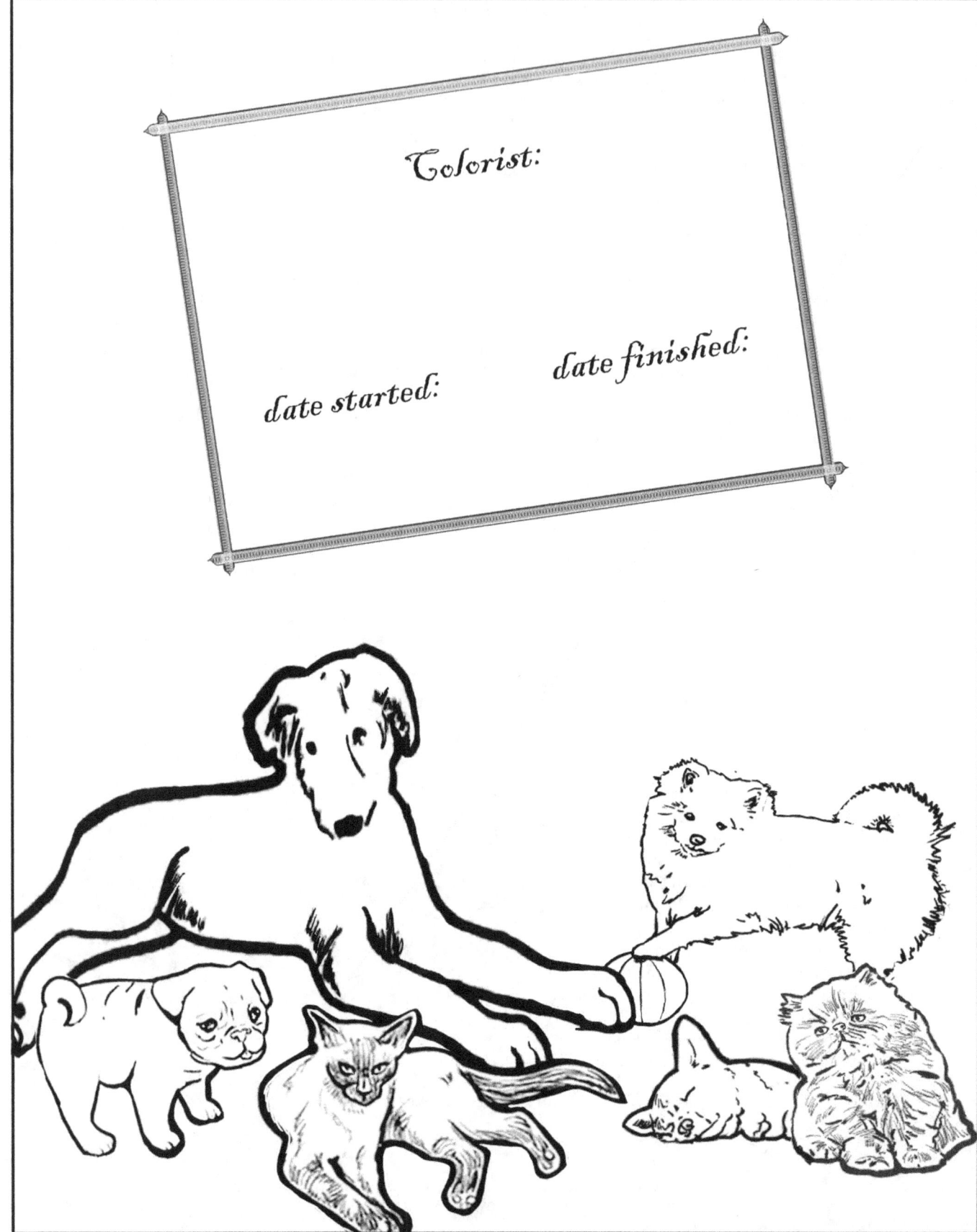

Colorist:

date started: date finished:

This page is to try your colors and techniques and media on. If you'd like coloring tutorials, contact me via www.facebook.com/agywilsonwork and let me know! Enjoy!

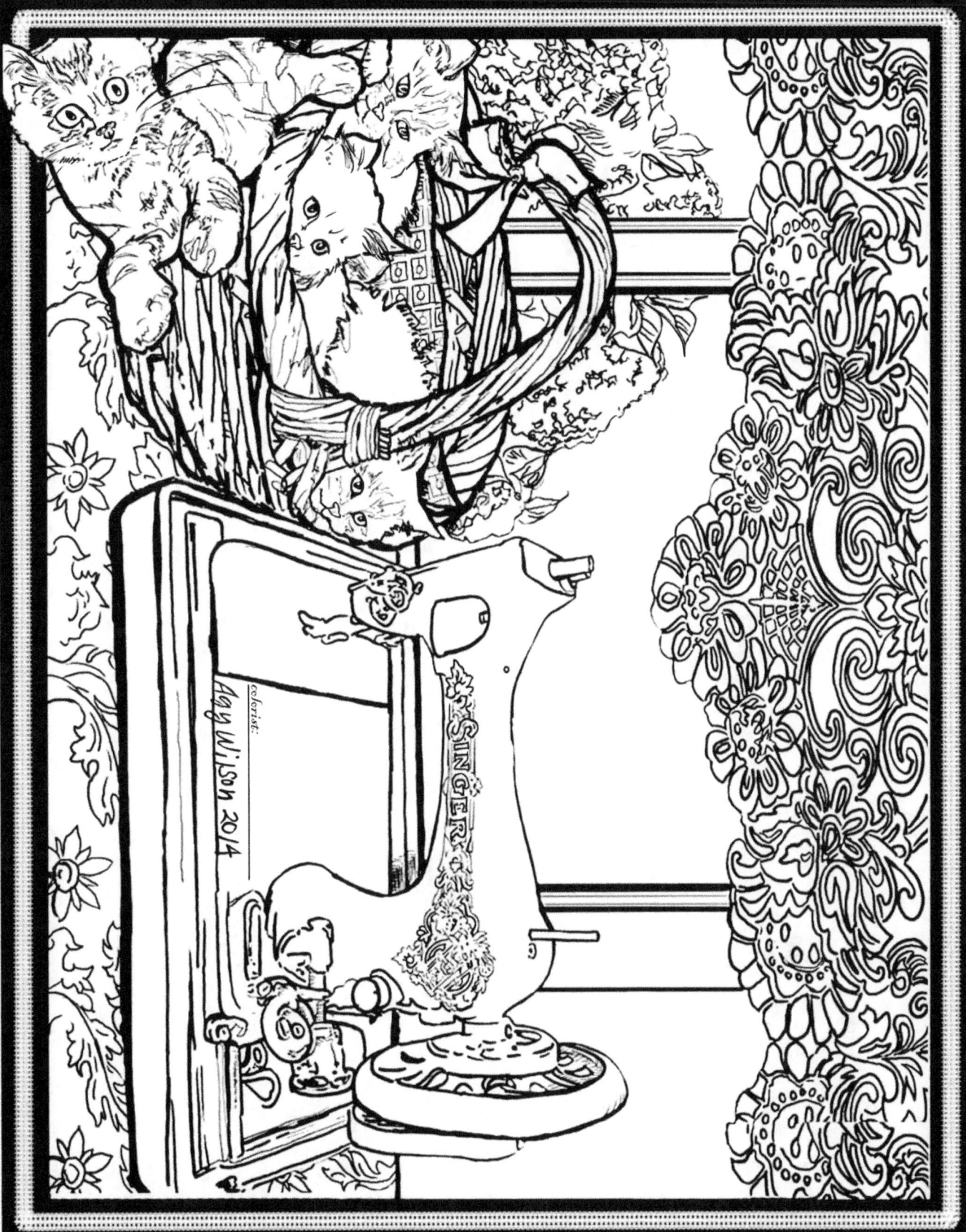

colorist: Agy Wilson 2014

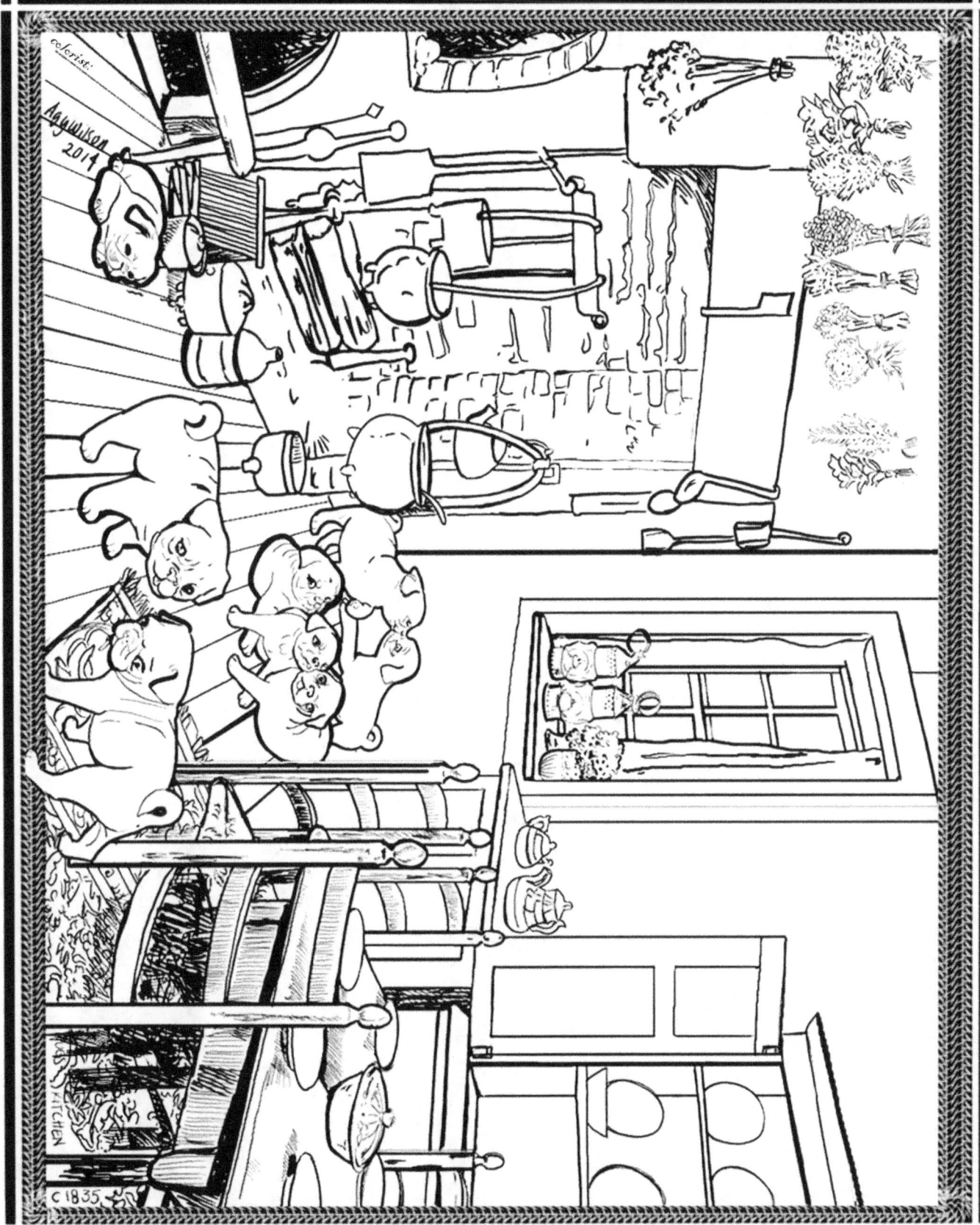

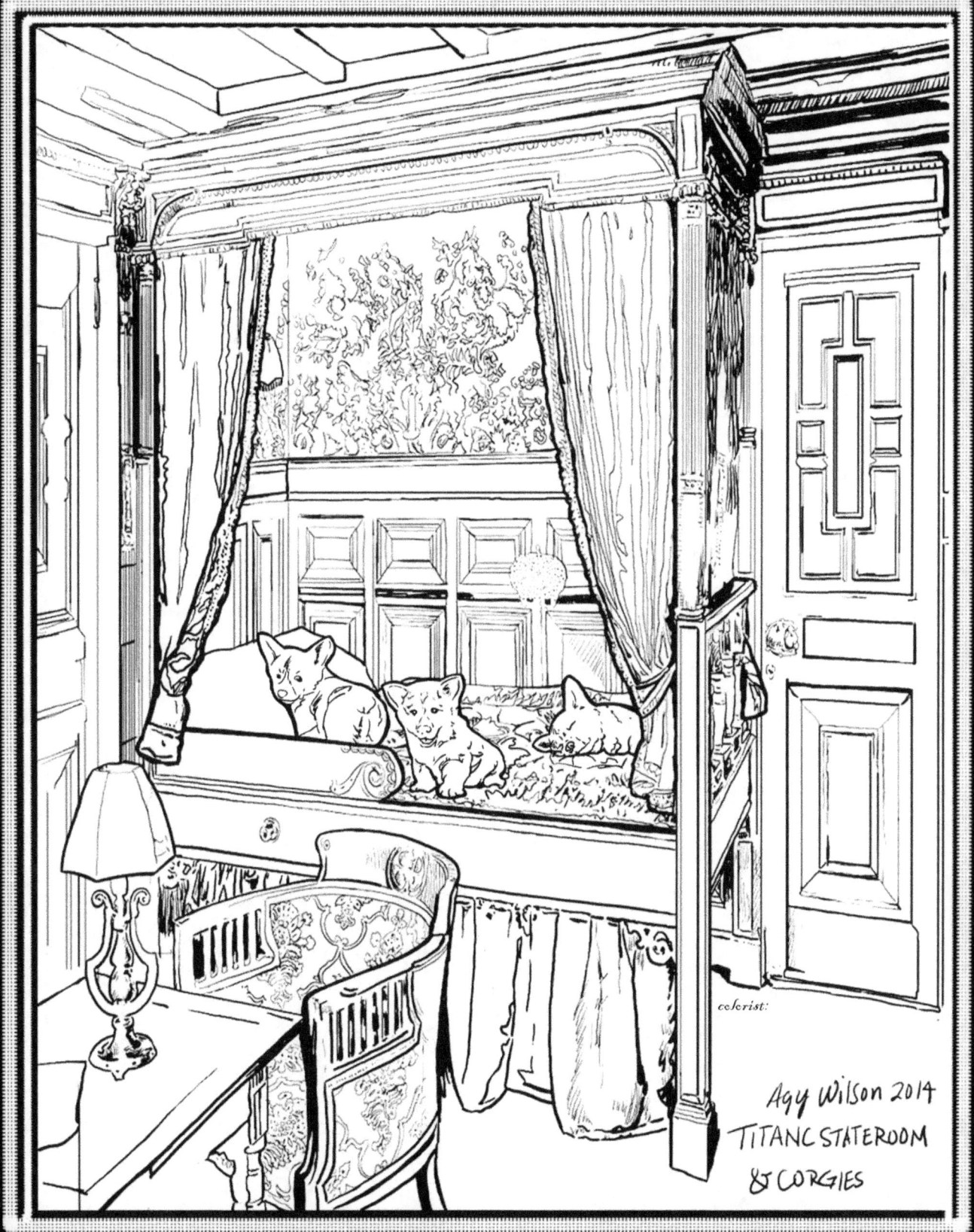

colorist:

Agy Wilson 2014
TITANC STATEROOM
& CORGIES

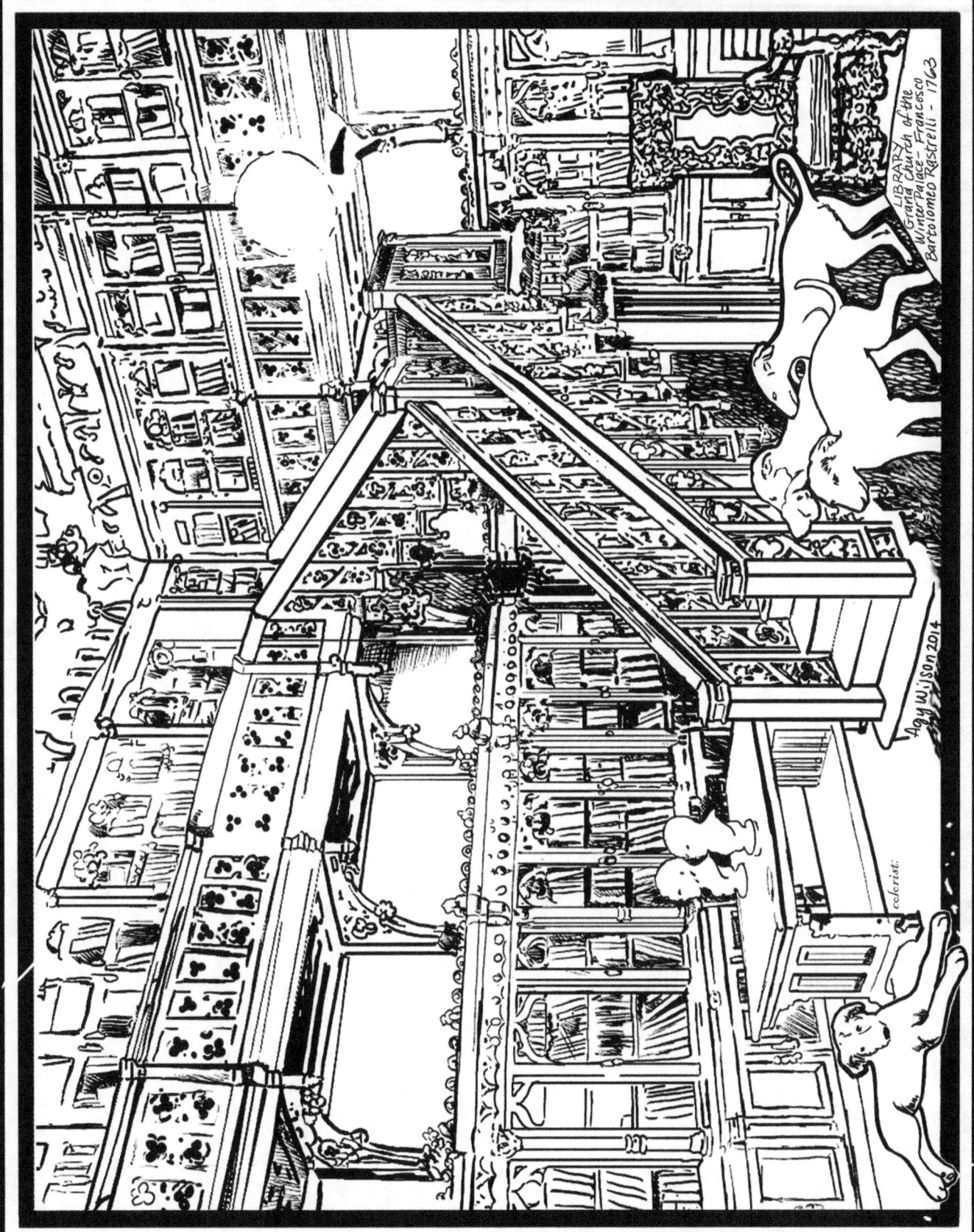

LIBRARY
Grand Church of the
Winter Palace— Francesco
Bartolomeo Rastrelli - 1763

Amy Wilson 2014

colorist:

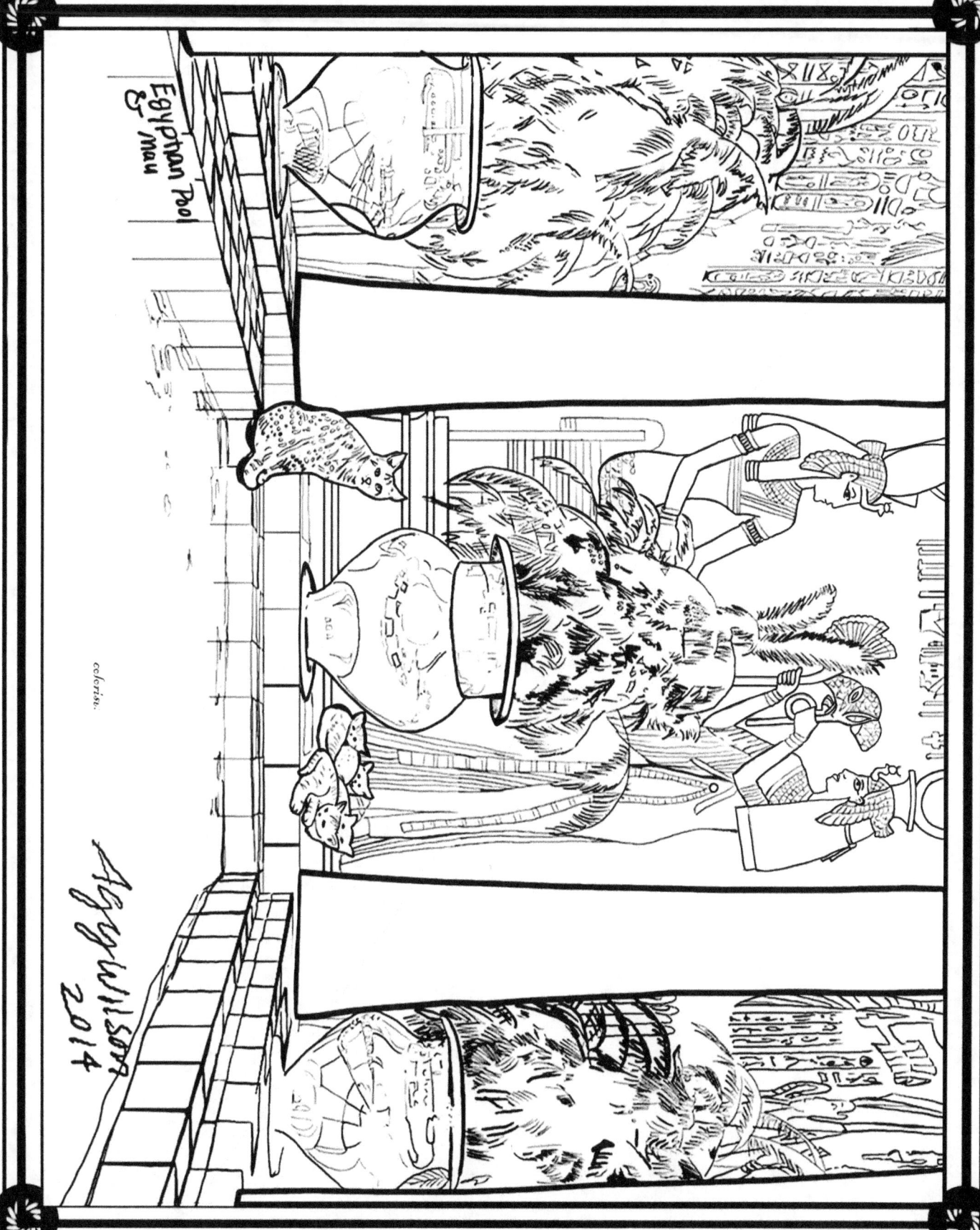

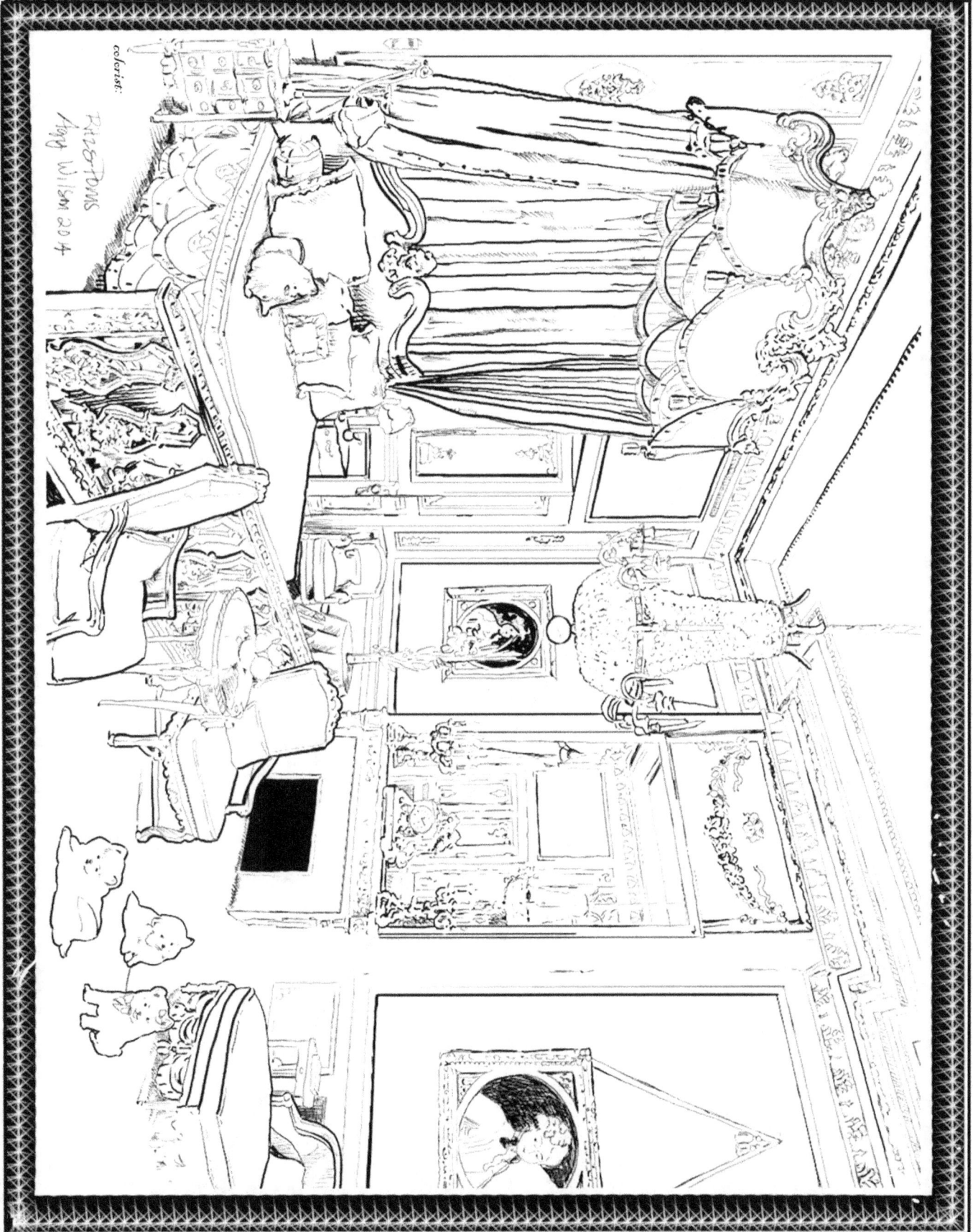

colorist:

Pins Dans
Amy Wilson 204

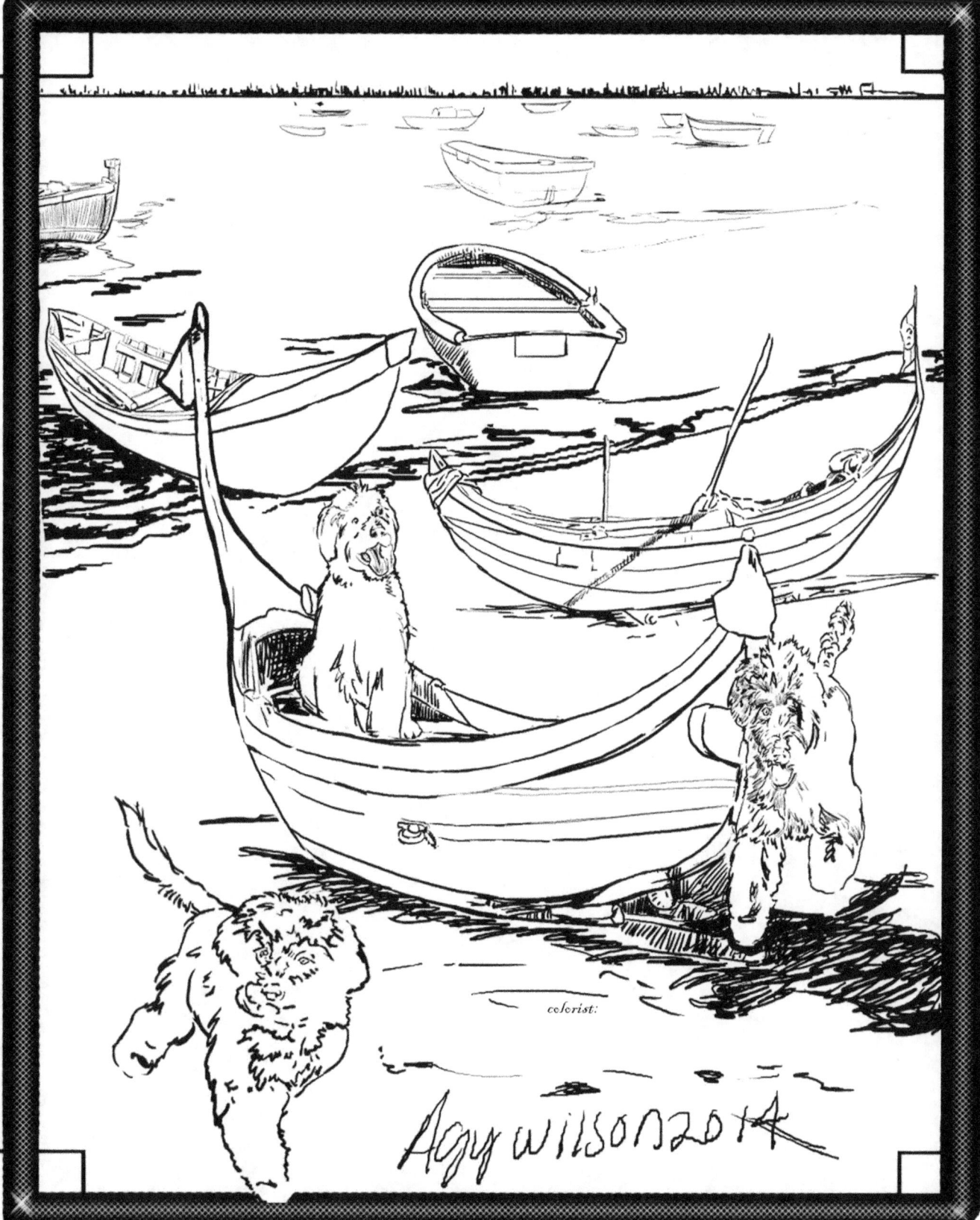

colorist:

agywilson2014

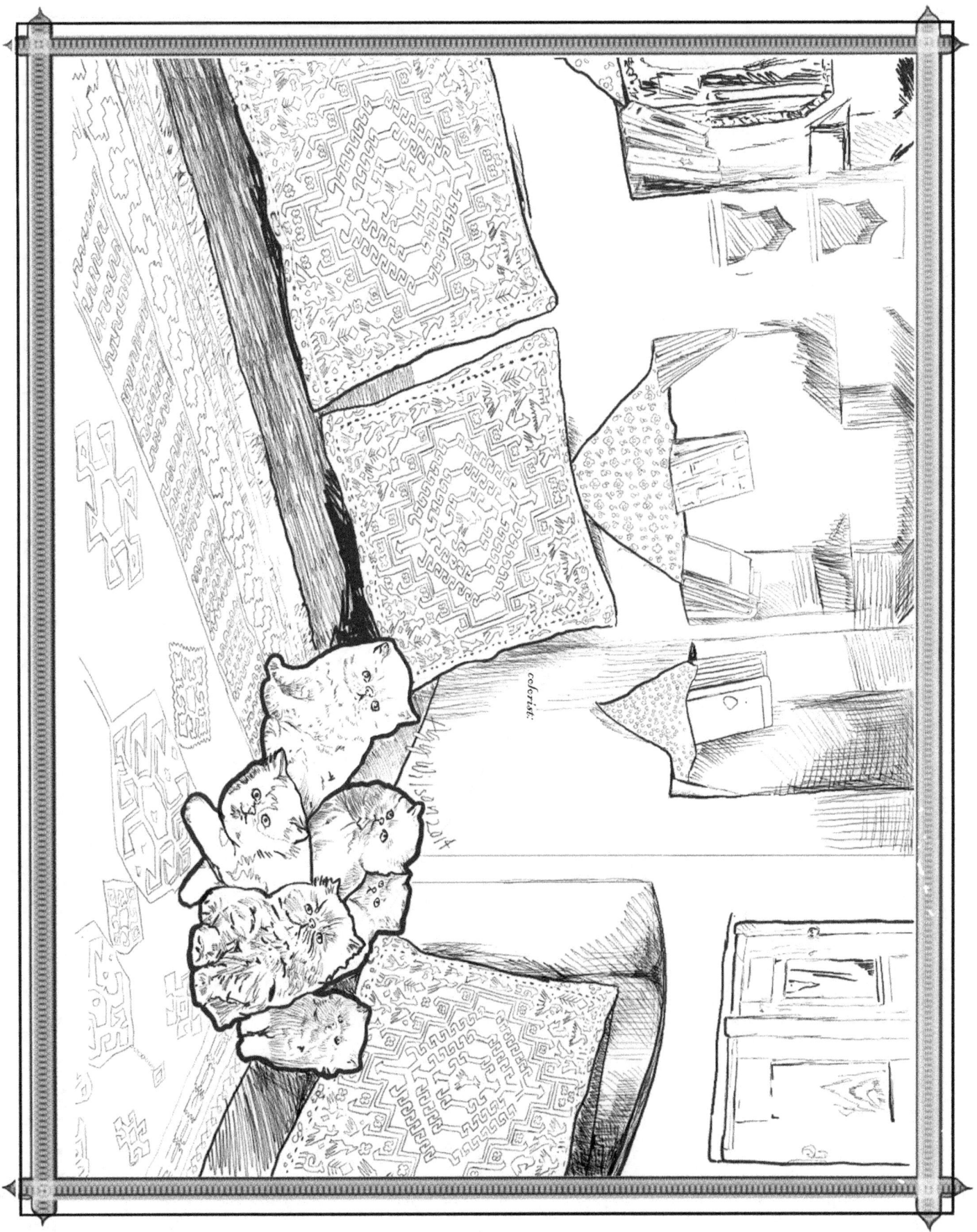

colorist:

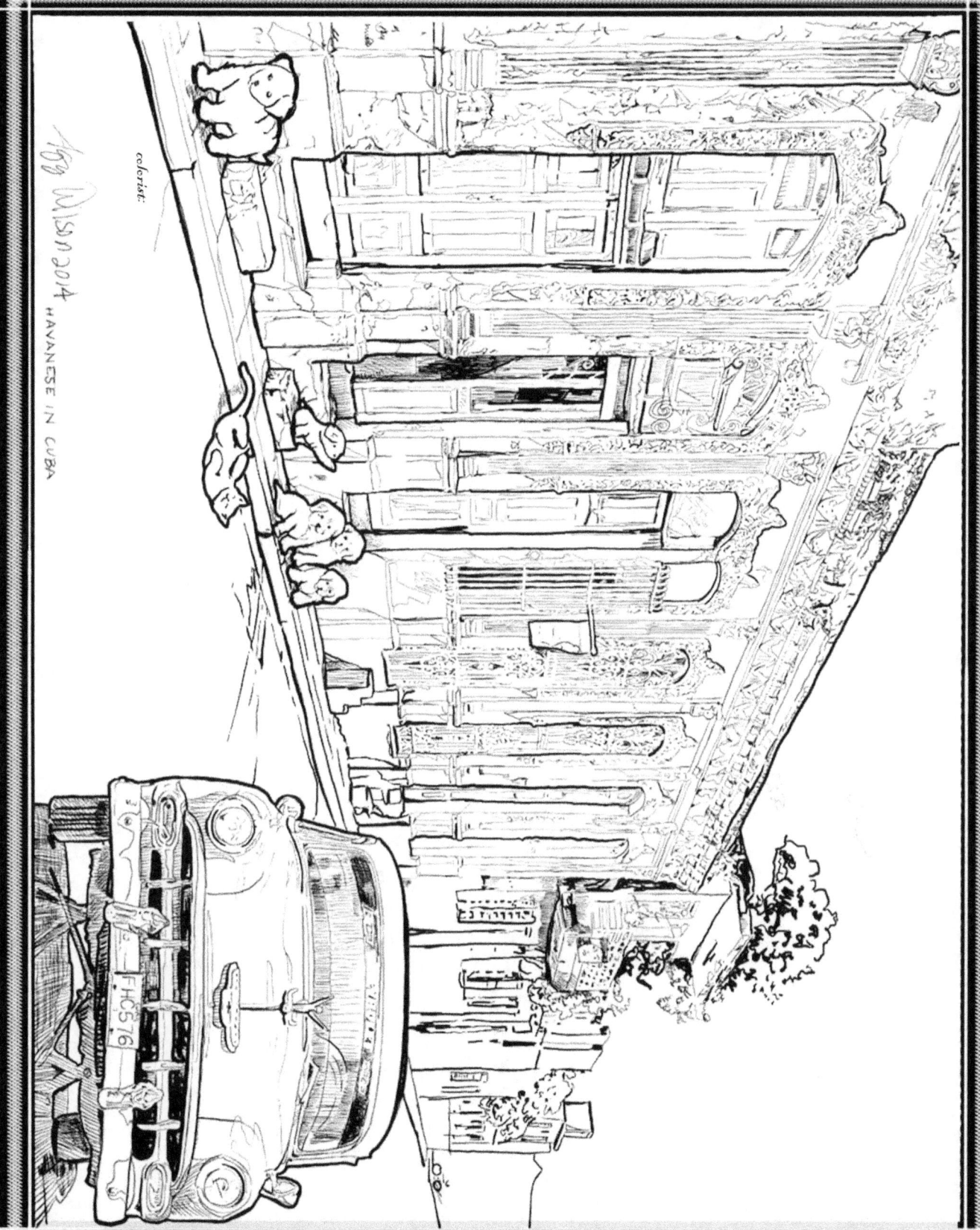

colorist:

HAVANESE IN CUBA

This page is to try your colors and techniques and media on. If you'd like coloring tutorials, contact me via www.facebook.com/agywilsonwork and let me know! Enjoy!

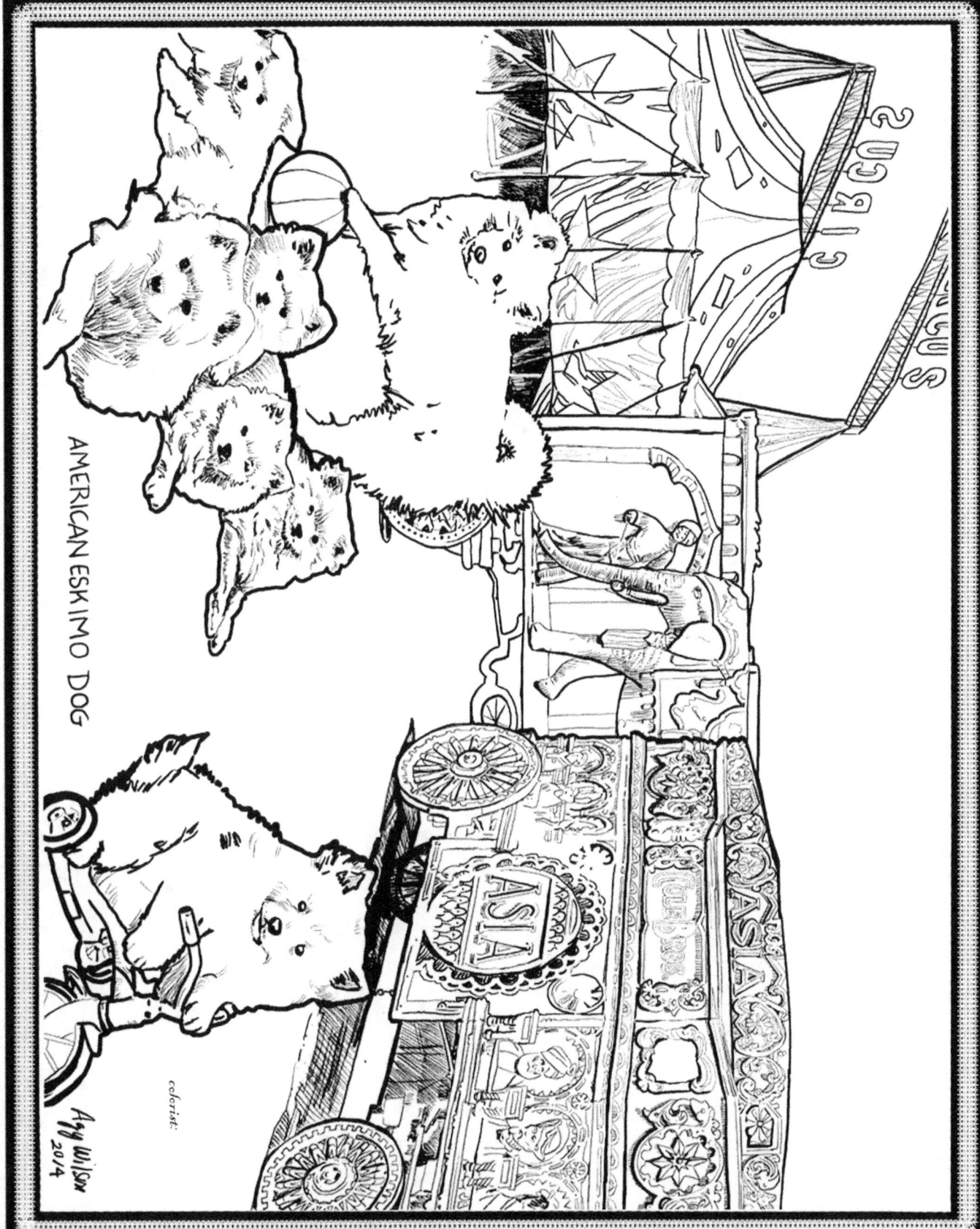

AMERICAN ESKIMO DOG

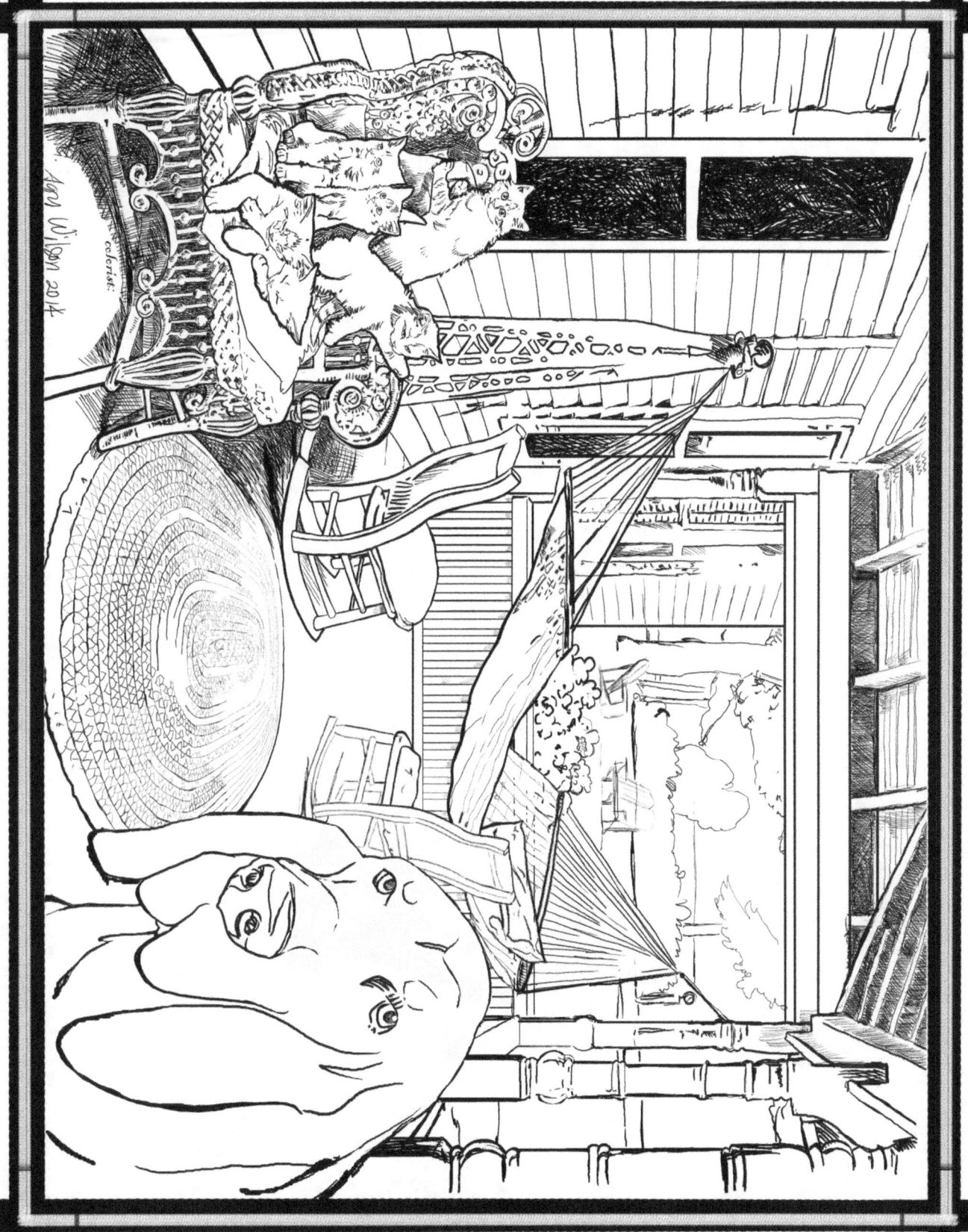

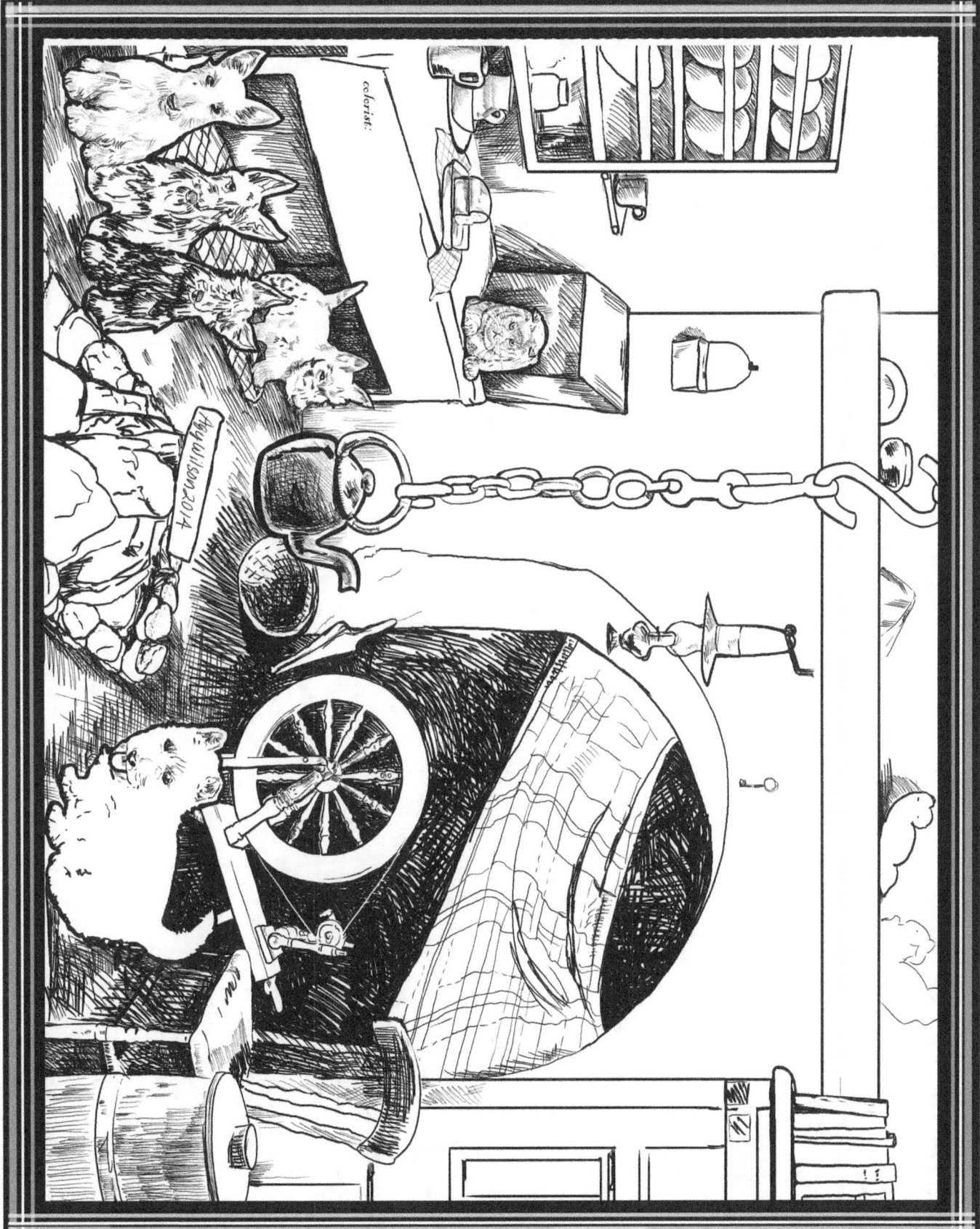

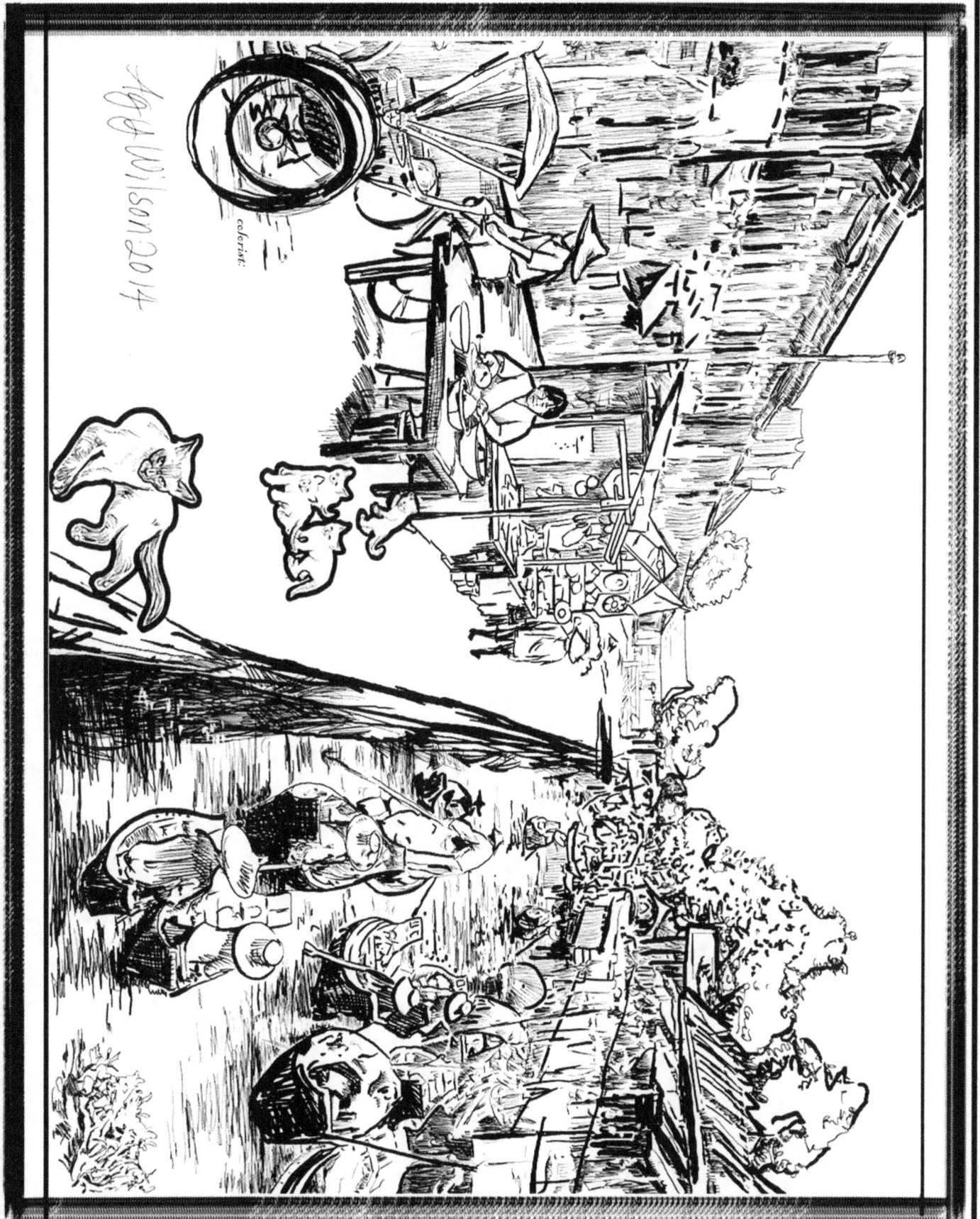

colorist:

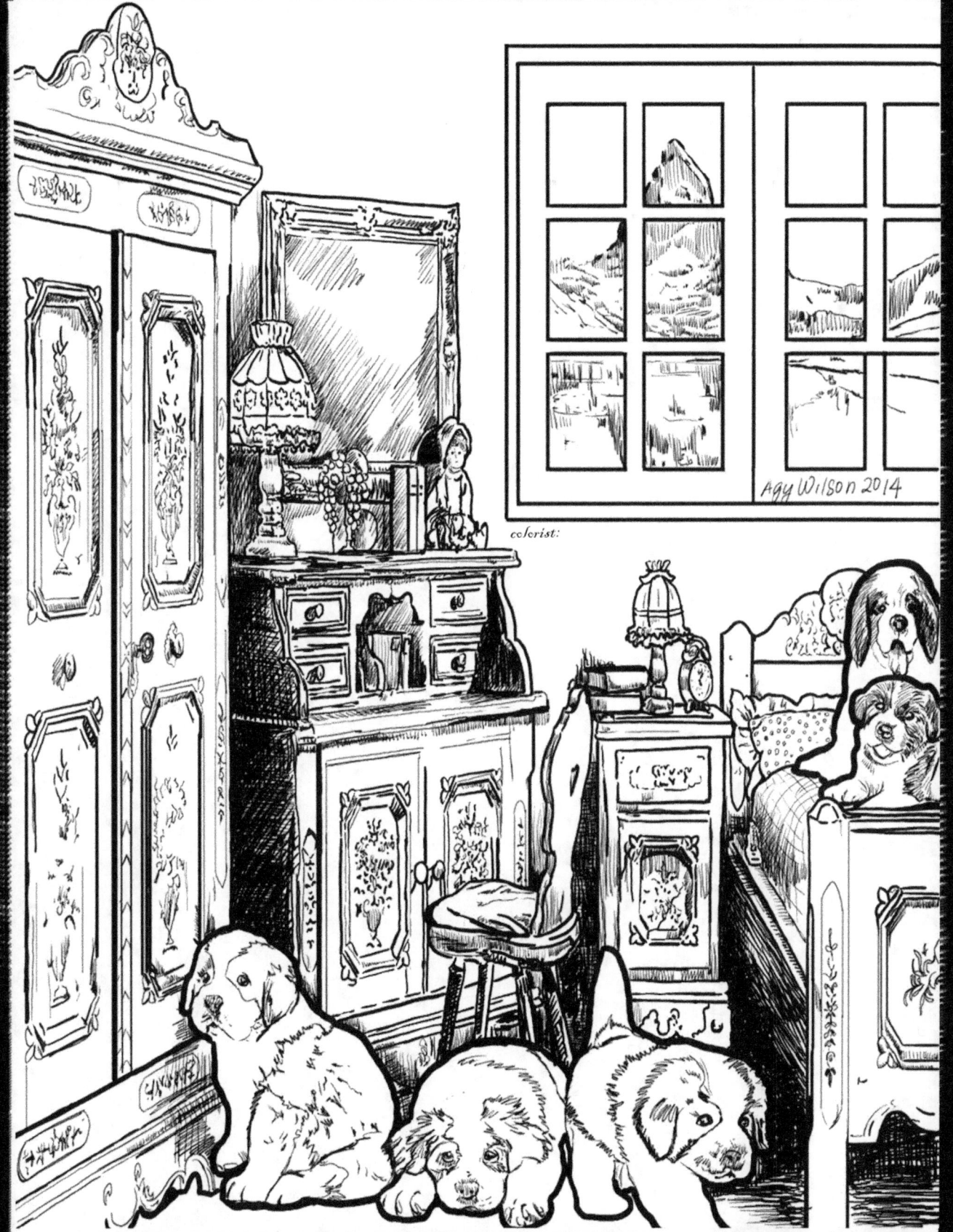

colorist:

Agy Wilson 2014

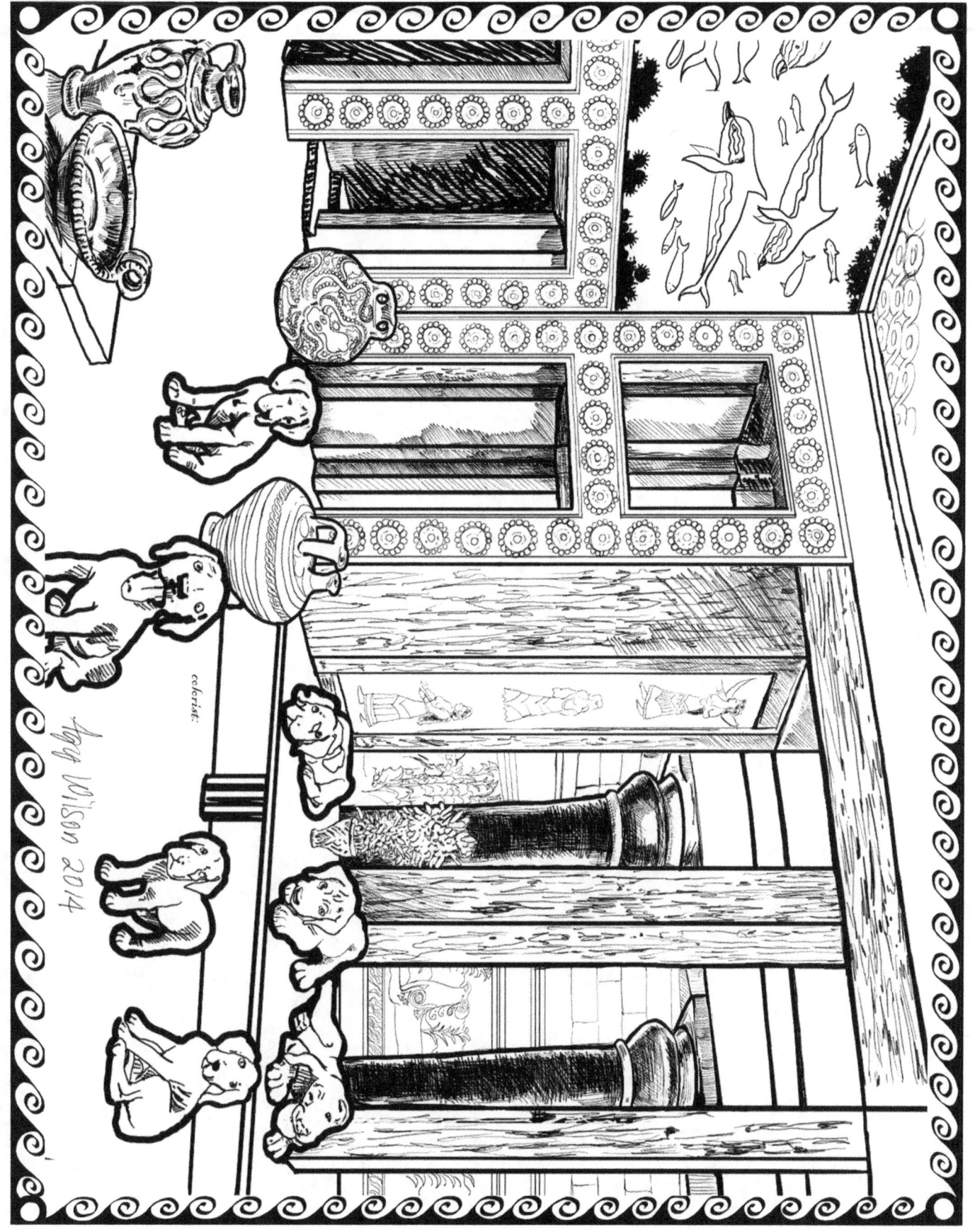

colorist:

Aga Wilson 2014

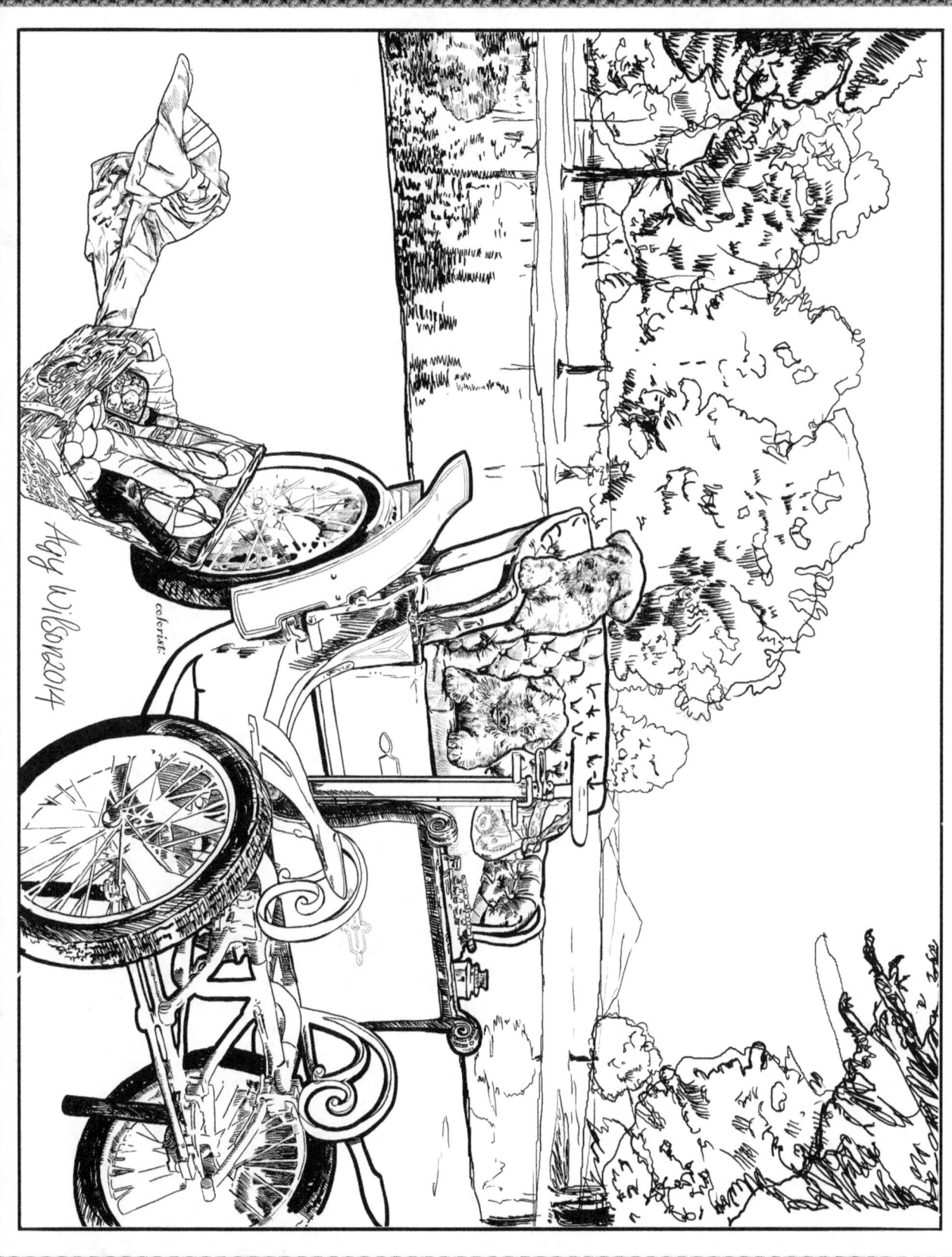

www.ingramcontent.com/pod-product-compliance
Lightning Source LLC
Chambersburg PA
CBHW080526190526
45169CB00008B/3063

* 9 7 8 1 5 2 3 8 8 9 5 6 3 *